New Directions for British Railways?

The Political Economy of Privatisation and Regulation

STEPHEN GLAISTER

and

TONY TRAVERS

*of the Greater London Group at
The London School of Economics and Political Science*

IEA
Institute of Economic Affairs
1993

First published in June 1993
by
THE INSTITUTE OF ECONOMIC AFFAIRS
2 Lord North Street, Westminster, London SW1P 3LB

© The Institute of Economic Affairs 1993

Current Controversies No.5

ISBN 0-255 36321-4

*The Institute gratefully acknowledges financial support for its publications
programme and other work from a generous benefaction by the late
Alec and Beryl Warren.*

Printed in Great Britain by
BOURNE PRESS LIMITED, BOURNEMOUTH

Set in Bembo 11 on 13 point

[2]

Contents

BOXES:

[4]

Foreword

ALL PRIVATISATIONS are difficult, but some are more difficult than others. Most of the state corporations which were privatised in the 1980s or early 1990s had been in government hands for at least forty years. As post-privatisation experience has demonstrated, they had been inefficient in their use of labour and other productive factors, the absence of competition had made management unimaginative and slow to innovate, and they had been unresponsive to consumer wants. Cross-subsidies abounded and most of the industries had been under considerable government pressure to take actions which were against their 'commercial' interests. Although many of the privatisation schemes were very imperfect – especially because they introduced relatively little competition at the outset – they did at least bring into the open costs which under state ownership had been concealed and force consideration of whether or not those costs could be justified.

The Government's railway privatisation scheme is likely to prove more difficult than most. That is not only because of the complexity of the industry and its long period of state ownership (and previous state supervision). Additional complications arise in the case of rail because the industry is in decline, receives very large subsidies and (in the South East in particular) is a form of transport which significantly affects the lives of many people and their families. Revealing the costs of individual operations within such a system may implicitly threaten widespread closures, service reductions and general re-organisation.

In *Current Controversies* No.5, Stephen Glaister and Tony Travers of the London School of Economics, lead us carefully through the government's proposals – which involve, *inter alia*, the establishment of a new infrastructure authority (RailTrack, which will remain state-owned initially), and a Franchising Director as well as a Regulator. As they point out, the degree of privatisation and competition will (initially, anyway) be small and there is a large element of re-regulation in the proposals. They stress that privatisation will release

[5]

new pressures '...because of increased openness about the condition, costs and benefits of the railways which may, in turn, lead to a debate about whether less (or more) should be spent on Britain's railway system' (Section 10, below, p.63).

They emphasise also the danger that government will still be tempted to intervene and they identify ways in which it will be able to do so: in their view, '...Ministerial intervention could seriously damage the benefits accruing from the new organisation of the railways' (Section 10, below, p.63).

Dr Glaister and Mr Travers produce many constructive proposals to help to provide a more efficient railway system which is better directed at meeting the demands of consumers. One of their most interesting conclusions (which conflicts with conventional wisdom) is that the best place to start extensive franchising is in the London area. Indeed, they conclude that '...complete privatisation of train operations and track ownership will be easier to achieve in the London area than elsewhere', despite the 'casual initial impression that the profitable InterCity business would be the easiest to privatise' (both quotations from Section 7, below, p.51).

The views expressed on this controversial subject are those of the authors, not of the Institute (which has no corporate view), its Trustees, Directors or Advisers. This *Current Controversies* is published in the hope of stimulating a constructive debate on the future of the railways under private ownership.

May 1993   COLIN ROBINSON
Editorial Director, Institute of Economic Affairs;
Professor of Economics, University of Surrey

The Authors

STEPHEN GLAISTER, PhD, is Cassel Reader in Economics with special reference to Transport at the London School of Economics.

He was a member of the Government's Advisory Committee on Trunk Road Assessment and he has been Specialist Advisor to the Parliamentary Select Committee on Transport. He was a non-executive director of London Regional Transport from 1984 until 1993.

He has acted as advisor to the Department of Transport on bus deregulation, and he developed models for the Department for the cost-benefit assessment of urban public transport subsidies. He has worked on urban transport evaluation for the World Bank. In December 1991 he published *Transport Options for London*, and in March 1993, *Meeting the Transport Needs of the City*, both with Tony Travers.

He has contributed widely to the journals and in books on transport. He is Managing Editor of the *Journal of Transport Economics and Policy*.

TONY TRAVERS is Director of Research of the Greater London Group at the LSE. He is a member of the Audit Commission. He has been a member of the Planning and Development Board of the Arts Council. He has published a number of books and reports on London, local government and transport, including *Meeting the Transport Needs of the City* (1993), and *The Impact of Population Size on Costs and Effectiveness in Local Government* (1993). He has acted as a consultant for many private and public organisations.

Acknowledgements

We are most grateful to Professor Michael Beesley, Charles Brown, Professor Sir Christopher Foster, Professor John Hibbs, Jan-Eric Nilsson, Professor Colin Robinson and others for comments on earlier drafts. The views expressed here are the personal views of the authors.

5 May 1993   S.G.
                                                                                T.T.

New Directions for British Railways?

The Political Economy of Privatisation and Regulation

STEPHEN GLAISTER and TONY TRAVERS

1. Background

THE ROLE OF THE GOVERNMENT has been a major issue throughout the history of railways in Britain. Nobody ever seems satisfied. Every 12 years, with remarkable regularity, the government of the day has demanded fundamental change. The current proposals[1] were introduced in 1992 and the Secretary of State has said that he expects them to take 12 years to carry out. 1980 saw the beginning of the process of creating separate British Rail Sector management.[2] 1968 was the year of Mrs Castle's monumental Transport Act which, among other things, initiated a response by the railways to competition from a deregulated road haulage industry, and attempted to isolate the costs and benefits of particular railway services and to fund loss-makers explicitly. The great Railway Modernisation Plan[3] dated from 1956. In 1944 plans were afoot to create the British Transport Commission which effectively nationalised the railways.[4] 1932 saw the preparation of the 1933 Road and Rail Traffic Act and the 1920 White Paper[5] introduced the legislation that amalgamated the railway companies into the Big Four under the 1921 Railways Act.

[1.] White Paper: *New Opportunities for the Railways*, Dept. of Transport, Cm.2012, London: HMSO, July 1992;
British Coal and British Rail (Transfer Proposals) Act 1993, London: HMSO, 1993;
Railways Bill, House of Commons Bill (117), London: HMSO, 1993.

[2.] R.B. Reid, *The Management of Railways by Business Sector*, British Railways Board, 1983.

[3.] British Transport Commission, *Proposals for the Railways*, Cmd.9880, London: HMSO, October 1956.

[4.] *Transport Act 1947*, London: HMSO, 1947. Section 2 (1) gave the Commission power 'to carry goods and passengers by rail, road and inland waterway within Great Britain'.

[5.] *Report on the General Revision of Railway Rates and Charges,* Cmd.1098, London: HMSO, 1920.

This paper considers a range of issues raised by the current proposals for change in railways generally described as 'privatisation'. The proposals are not a deregulation because the railways are, to a large extent, already deregulated. Nor are they a privatisation in the sense that the public has come to understand the term: the state will continue wholly to own the infrastructure assets, at least for a period. State subsidy will continue to be paid and this will bring with it a tendency - indeed, a responsibility - for the state to continue to intervene.

Improving Efficiency via Franchising

In general we support proposals to introduce more market discipline into the operation of railways, which is a primary objective. There is a good prospect that improved costing will reveal inefficiencies which can be eliminated by introducing the incentives created by genuine contracting and other market mechanisms. Franchising, which is proposed, can create competition amongst operators and raise productivity whilst improving service quality, as the experience with buses in London has illustrated. The franchising process provides a framework in which to achieve a more considered and rational pattern of financial support for rail services. Our purpose is not to undermine the proposals, but to analyse the decisions that must be made by the several newly-created bodies and the pressures they are likely to face.

In our view, the dangers to be avoided are as follows. One is that the public will oppose the proposals if their true nature is not successfully communicated. The details of what is proposed are only slowly becoming visible. On the basis of what has been announced, the final outcome for the industry could be anywhere on a spectrum of possibilities. Another problem is that the proposals may be clouded by changes made during the passage of the legislation. A further danger is that the benefits of the policy might be compromised by continued, or even increased, exposure to the vagaries of central government interference and inter-departmental conflict which railway managers have found disruptive and have come to resent so much in the past.

There are three separate (though related) issues which should be distinguished. The *first* is whether or not there has been under-funding of investment in existing physical assets and, if so, how that is to be rectified. The *second* is the future total level of state subsidy and therefore the commensurate size of the railway in the future. The *third* is the 'privatisation' policy itself – which is a change in the organisation, accounting, ownership and procurement of train services. It is easy for an uninformed public and opposed vested interests to confuse these issues. For instance, people sometimes assume that introducing private profit incentives into train operations is the same thing as removing state subsidy to the railway. It is not.

We emphasise the political nature of rail privatisation and, most particularly, the difference between rail privatisation and earlier privatisations. In brief, people have an unusual and romantic attachment to railways, they are concerned about changes that affect their locality (and possibly their property prices), and they want security of supply and the continuation of through-ticketing arrangements. Yet much of the industry appears fundamentally unprofitable, with doubtful prospects for improvement. This leaves much less room for manœuvre than in other privatisations. Unless there is clarity over principles and over the strategy of presentation, major political problems could ensue.

If separate accounting systems for identified pieces of track and individual train operations are introduced, this will inevitably expose to the public gaze a much clearer picture of existing patterns of cross-subsidy. This will stimulate a healthy and much better informed debate, which will centre on the question of keeping open services which make large losses. An unspoken function of the present system is to hide many of these problems by averaging and bundling. There are bound to be services which will be shown by separate accounting to be very highly subsidised and will therefore be subject to commercial pressures. Others will be shown to be more profitable than expected. Much needs to be done to achieve the requisite improvement in information.

Under the proposals,[1] a large proportion of the activities necessary

[1.] See note 1, above, page 9.

in producing rail services are to remain initially in the public sector. One major part of the industry will stay as a conventional nationalised industry and another will be a wholly state-owned company. In the longer term one of these, the track authority, may be in a position to take the lead on the way the industry develops. There will be powers to privatise the whole industry in due course. Not one but two new offices will be set up—a regulator and a service procurer. Four different kinds of 'producer' will exist. The Government is taking special precautions so that it can keep direct control of withdrawals of service. These arrangements will create the opportunity, and may encourage the Government to monitor, direct and generally interfere in a manner which is familiar to any nationalised industry board.

Moreover, it is possible for the state to pay subsidy for several distinct reasons. The Government has not given up its ability to control the industry; it has adopted the belt-and-braces approach of devolving responsibilities whilst reserving the powers to intervene formally and informally.

Flexibility of the Current Proposals

The proposals as they now stand are inherently flexible. Franchising can proceed quickly or slowly depending on the response of the market and on how policy and funding develop. There is no need to insist on any one standard form of contract arrangement, as the Government has recognised. The railway is a large and diverse set of services and different structures must be created to suit the differing circumstances. Sometimes it will be appropriate to keep infrastructure and operations vertically integrated: for instance, where a piece of infrastructure exists only for the benefit of one service, which is for the benefit of one end-user. At the other extreme there will be operations using spare capacity left over from the activities of other users. It will be sensible to protect this flexibility and to allow the system to evolve, rather than attempting to decide the structures *ab initio*. It is crucial that the opportunity is created for those involved to learn the best way of proceeding; to allow the policy to evolve; and not to create undesirable precedents early on in the process.

Previous privatisations were deliberately designed to remove industries from beyond the immediate reach of government. There was a genuine and largely successful attempt to free the industries from state interference. The systems of regulation in these industries are to safeguard the 'public interest' and they have proved able to withstand attempts at government meddling. In the case of railways, however, the industry may end up under *more* direct control than at present: the British Railways Board, by virtue of its size and scope, does have a degree of independence. Part of the motivation for the change in the arrangements is the view that, isolated from competitive disciplines, this independence has been misused to acquiesce in a high degree of inefficiency.

More complete privatisation would make the new industry more immune from interference but the existence of subsidy will inevitably slow change. The Government may be unable to resist political pressures to intervene in the market or quasi-market mechanisms that are to be created, thus risking undermining the achievements and improvements which privatisation could bring.

2. An Outline of the Industry

BRITISH RAIL is presently organised into seven businesses, together with a relatively small Group Headquarters and an internal 'Services' business.

• InterCity runs mainline express passenger services between major centres. It has several profit centres (such as the East and West Coast Mainlines, the Great Western, and so on), most of which correspond to the original mainline railway companies.

• Network SouthEast (NSE) operates passenger services in the South-East region of England. It operates most of the commuter rail services into London, except for shorter-distance routes operated by London Underground; some commuters use InterCity services. NSE also operates local services over a large area, many of which are akin to the rural services of Regional Railways. It has nine profit centres.

• Regional Railways operate most of the remaining passenger services, which range from commuter flows into conurbations to deep rural services. There are five profit centres, one of which (Scotrail) operates most rail services in Scotland.

[13]

- The remaining profit centres are European Passenger Services, two freight businesses (Trainload Freight and Railfreight Distribution) and Parcels.

- Intercity and Freight are directed to operate at a profit. A block grant (the Public Service Obligation (PSO) grant) is given to the British Railways Board in respect of Network SouthEast and Regional Railways.

1991-92 A Bad Year for British Rail

Table 1 shows operating results by Sector (the predecessors of the Businesses) in 1990-91 and corresponding surpluses and losses for 1991-92. These results rely on a particular cost allocation convention - the prime user system explained below. In 1990-91 InterCity succeeded in making an operating profit, but Freight did not. The bulk of the subsidy went to Regional Railways. The following year was a bad one for the railways, as the Table shows, since the industry's fortunes are closely tied to those of the economy. InterCity broke even, Network SouthEast lost £351 million and Regional Railways lost £622 million. Freight lost £51 million and parcels lost £35 million.

The External Financing Limit (EFL) is the total amount of money a nationalised industry is allowed to spend in any one year from external sources: that is, in the case of British Rail, in addition to fares income, income from property sales and from miscellaneous sources. It is one of the main components of the Government's control process. Figure 1 shows the EFLs at 1992 prices from 1986-87 to 1992-93, together with the three-year forward commitment announced in the Autumn Statement in November 1992.

External funding had been falling during the mid-1980s, but it rose at the turn of the decade because of falling revenues, falling property sales income and increasing investment requirements (largely to fund the investment associated with the Channel Tunnel). According to forecasts, the intention is that external funding should more than halve over the next three years.

[cont'd on p. 17]

TABLE 1

British Rail Sector Results, 1990–91 and 1991–92

| | The Passenger Railway | | | The Freight Railway | | |
| | The Subsidised Railway | | | The Commercial Railway | | |
	Network South East	Regional Railways	InterCity	Trainload Freight	Railfreight Distrib'n	Parcels
Revenue* (£million) 1990–91	998·3	303·7	851·2	509·5	172·8	115·8
Costs+ (£million) 1990–91	1,153·2	807·1	801·5	410·8	325·1	41·6
Revenue/Cost Ratio 1990–91	0·87	0·38	1·06	1·24	0·53	0·82
Surplus (loss) before Subsidy (£million) 1990–91	(155)	(503)	50	99	(152)	(25·8)
Surplus (loss) before Subsidy (£million) 1991–92	(351)	(622)	2	(51)		(35)

*Turnover excluding subsidy.

+Excludes interest.

Source: British Railways Board Annual Report and Accounts 1990/91, p.38; Dodgson (1992); and Dept. of Transport, *The Government's Expenditure Plans for Transport, 1993-94 to 1995-96*, Cm. 2206, London: HMSO, 1993.

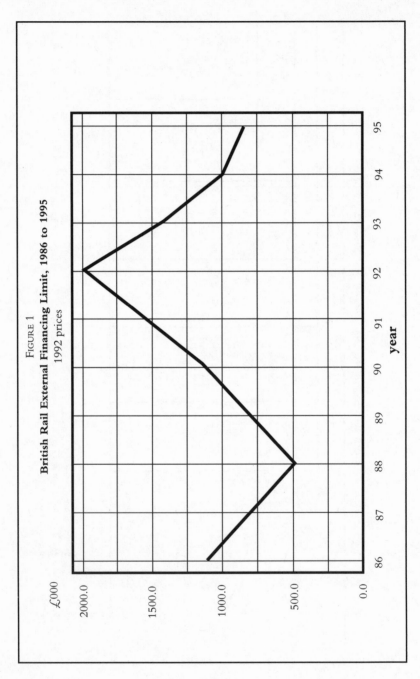

FIGURE 1
British Rail External Financing Limit, 1986 to 1995
1992 prices

£000

Variations in Productive Performance

Table 2 shows the Government's official summary statistics on productivity from 1986-87 to 1990-91. Nash and Preston (1992) report that the ratio of annual train operating revenue to track miles increased from £96·8 per mile in 1985-86 to £125·6 per mile in 1990-91 (at 1990-91 prices), an improvement of 30 per cent. Annual track, signal and telecommunication costs per track mile have been reduced from £42,759 to £34,937, an improvement of 18 per cent.

TABLE 2
British Rail Productivity, 1986-87 to 1990-91

	86-87	87-88	88-89	89-90	90-91
Total operating expenses per train mile (£s) (1990/91 prices)[1]	14·42	14·62	13·30	13·34	13·28
Train miles per member of staff	1,835	1,918	2,074	2,113	2,114
Revenue per £1,000 gross paybill costs (£)	1,478	1,594	1,672	1,615	1,574
PSO grant per supported passenger mile (pence) (1990/91 prices)[1]	5·08	5·06	5·30	4·73	5·16

[1] Deflated by GDP.

Source: Dept. of Transport, *The Government's Expenditure Plans for Transport, 1992-93 to 1994-95*, Cm. 1907, London: HMSO, 1992.

There is, of course, considerable variation in economic performance of different services within sectors. One of the principal sources of variation is the nature of the competition railways face on different routes. InterCity has more than 80 per cent of the business travel market between London and Leeds, about 60 per cent to Manchester, 15 per cent to Glasgow and 10 per cent to Aberdeen. Another source of variation is the density of total traffic on the routes. Regional Railways have routes where the total market is small, or the total market is large but the private car has left a small part of it to public transport.

[17]

The results of the differing commercial objectives and differing competitive environments of the main passenger sectors can usefully be summarised in the fares elasticities that they face (Table 3). The fares elasticity is defined as the percentage change in patronage caused by a 1 per cent change in fare. If the elasticity is less than 1 ('inelastic'), then raising fares will raise revenue, but if it is greater than 1 ('elastic'), raising fares will reduce revenue. In both cases raising fares will reduce patronage. The indications given in Table 3 are drawn from experience of the impact of fares changes within a few months of the change. Response is likely to be substantially greater over a period of years during which people are likely to adjust their places of work and home, and other land uses will have had time to respond.

TABLE 3
Fares Elasticities

	InterCity	NSE	Regional Railways
Standard Class			
Commuting	<<1	<<1	<1
Business	<1	<1	<1
Personal business	>1	<1	1
Leisure	>>1	>1	>>1
First Class	<1	<1	<1

Key: << 1: substantially less than 1
< 1: less than 1
> 1: greater than 1
>> 1: substantially greater than 1

The Table indicates that most of NSE's markets are inelastic, as a result of relatively low fares and the degree of monopoly power arising from the inherent advantages that rail has over road for passengers in the London region. As we have noted, NSE consists of far more than the London-centred market. Parts of it are more akin to Regional Railways and they probably exhibit similar fares elasticities.

InterCity and Regional leisure markets are more elastic because of the competition presented by other modes, and because of the success the operators have had in setting commercial, net-revenue-maximising fares. There is little new revenue to be had in these markets by raising fares.

Reduced Pressure of Economic Regulation

Much economic regulation was developed in the context of railways.[1] But, since the mid-1950s, British Railways have been progressively relieved of almost all economic regulation. They now enjoy more freedom in price setting and choice of who to serve and at what level of service than do private industries, with two main exceptions. *First,* the railways have found it virtually impossible to withdraw completely any existing passenger services because of refusal by Ministers to give consent. *Second,* fares are held below profit-maximising levels in certain rail commuter markets (notably in the London area) by an informal but powerful system of regulation which results from the Railways Board responding to pressure from the Department of Transport.

As a generalisation, passenger fares are determined in one of two ways. Either they are set at the railway's estimate of the profit-maximising level in a competitive market where it has little monopoly power, or, for social and political reasons, they are constrained to be substantially below the profit-maximising level in markets where the railway has substantial monopoly power.

Variation in quality is another source of heterogeneity in rail markets. Travel is a commodity for which quality is perceived as important by passengers. Quality has several dimensions. For rail these include speed, frequency of service, reliability, crowding, ease of interchange, rolling stock cleanliness and quality, and ease of access to the rail system. British Rail have estimates of the effects of changing these attributes on demand at the broad level of detail indicated in Table 3. In future, monitoring of service quality, the effects of service quality on demand and the effects of price on demand will all be required at a much finer level of detail.

Rail travel - both passenger and freight - is intimately related to the general volume of activity in the economy, and rail volume is therefore sensitive to measures of economic activity, like gross domestic

[1] See Foster (1992), for an excellent survey.

product (GDP), consumer incomes or retail sales. Over the decades it is this relationship that is dominant in determining the level of rail demand. The future state of the economy will be just as important a determinant of the fortunes of the rail industry as the outcome of the privatisation debate, and the interaction of these factors could influence the politics of rail privatisation.

3. The Main Actors

THE INTENDED STRUCTURE is set out in the White Paper (Cm.2012, DoT, 1992a), in the Railways Bill and in *Gaining Access to the Railway Network, the Government's Proposals* (DoT, 1993).

RailTrack: will stay within the public sector in the short term. It will be a 'GoCo', a company under the provisions of the Companies Act 1985 with all the issued shares held by the Secretary of State, an arrangement similar to that which applies to London Buses Ltd. and London Underground Ltd., which are technically subsidiaries of London Regional Transport under the Companies Act. The White Paper says that

> 'In the longer term the Government would like to see the private sector owning as much as possible of the railway. Powers will therefore be taken to allow the future privatisation of all BR track and operations' (Cm.2012, para.18).

RailTrack will operate, maintain and invest in the fixed infrastructure, principally track and signalling. It will be responsible for defining train paths and timetabling them. It will be given the financial objective to break even after earning a defined rate of return on capital, recovering the bulk of its costs through charges to users of all kinds (though no estimate has been published of the proportion of revenues that might come from alternative sources). The Secretary of State will retain the power to give capital grants direct to RailTrack:

> 'The Government is also ready to provide direct support for infrastructure investment projects which, although not earning an adequate rate of return, provide a satisfactory cost/benefit return when wider benefits are considered.' (Cm.2012, para.43.)

This statement is particularly interesting in that it sanctions the justification of specific rail infrastructure investments by means of

[20]

cost/benefit assessments, as with trunk roads for many years.

If RailTrack were to remain within the standard public expenditure control process, it would be caught within the unpredictable mêlée of national funding decisions which has made funding of British Rail and London Transport so erratic in recent years.[1] The Government is considering how to avoid such problems. RailTrack will contract out its own support functions, for example, track maintenance, where that offers value for money (Cm.2012, para. 24).

RailTrack's point of departure will be the existing timetable. Over time it is envisaged that varying pressures from the different markets to which it sells capacity will lead to changes. Conflicts between demands by freight services and passenger services, and between local and express services, will be resolved by selling train paths to those willing to pay most. What paths can be defined depends, amongst other things, on the speed of the trains using them. Hence the design of the timetable, which has to be completed in advance of operation and must anticipate which are likely to be the most remunerative paths. These estimates will have to be refined in an iterative process as actual market pressures are revealed.

The Franchising Director: will define services, singly or in bundles, which will be offered to independent train operators under competitive tender. The successful bid may be positive or negative, depending upon the view the market takes of the profitability of the bundle. It will generally be open to the bidder to decide his own scale of charges to passengers, although the Franchising Director may control fares in certain circumstances. The contract for which a bid is made will specify the services to be offered; the Franchising Director will have 'booked' the appropriate train paths with RailTrack in advance on known terms. The tariff will have two parts: a fixed access charge and a charge related to the volume of usage. It may vary between peak and off-peak periods.

The Government intends that eventually it will pass all financial support for the railways through the Franchising Director with the exception of certain capital grants. It will be the Franchising Director's responsibility to determine the level of subsidy required to maintain

[1] Described in detail in Glaister and Travers (1993).

[21]

each service. If a bundle is let for a positive bid the monies received will be paid into the Consolidated Fund (that is, to the Exchequer). Bundles let at a negative bid will be paid for out of the Franchising Director's budget which will be set by the Secretary of State for Transport.[1] In this way most of the money going to subsidise franchised train operations will be explicitly voted by Parliament.

The Franchising Director will be set objectives by and be answerable to the Secretary of State, who will also set a budget.[2] These objectives are not explicitly set out in the Bill, apart from a duty to achieve the objectives economically and efficiently. He will therefore be, to all intents and purposes, in the same position as a nationalised industry and subject to similar pressures with all the attendant risks of short-term political intervention.

The Regulator: is to be established as an independent entity, with several functions. He will issue licences to operators (or grant exemptions to the requirement to be licensed). He will resolve disputes, prevent anti-competitive practices in the setting of charges and the making of agreements between the active parties. He will oversee the agreements giving train service operators access to infrastructure, the agreements between the franchised service operators and the Franchising Director, and the operation of fares control formulae which may be set as licence conditions on operators. He will approve the charging régime set by RailTrack for the use of the infrastructure. The Bill (clause 4) sets the Secretary of State and the Regulator common duties:

- to protect the interests of users;

- to promote the use of the railway network;

- to promote efficiency and economy;

- to promote competition;

- to promote through-ticketing;

and to enable rail service providers to plan their businesses with a reasonable degree of assurance.

1. *Railways Bill 1993*, clause 27.
2. *Ibid.*, clause 5.

The Regulator can insist on an independent operator gaining access to the track on reasonable terms, including services in direct competition with those on franchise contracts - although the Government has said that it may wish to restrict this direct competition in the early stages to ease the letting of the first franchises.[1] Under an amendment to the original Bill, the Regulator will also be under a duty to take into account any guidance given to him by the Secretary of State until the end of 1996.

The Regulator will deal with up to 10 Rail Users' Consultative Committees and a Central Rail Users' Committee. He will receive proposals from the Franchising Director for service closures and consider them, possibly in the forum of a public inquiry. If the Regulator decides on closure, appeals may be made to the Secretary of State who will have power to pay direct subsidy to forestall closure. The Regulator will also have the power to undertake the functions of the Director General of Fair Trading in respect of the railway industry.

As is normal in this kind of legislation, the Secretary of State (that is, *any* Secretary of State) retains the power to exempt operators and services from designations or requirements stipulated by either the Regulator or the Franchising Director. The main reason is to ensure the ability to exempt London Underground services.

British Rail operations and infrastructure services: will continue for a period - possibly for several years - while services are progressively franchised and infrastructure is transferred. The Government is keen to have complete franchising as soon as possible. Operations will be separate from RailTrack and it will have a new and separate management structure. The Government will continue to exercise the same régime of normal public sector scrutiny as now. It will pay PSO grant for the residual services.

RailTrack will 'buy in' most of its services, such as infrastructure maintenance, signalling repairs, investment, and so on, initially from British Rail and, over time, from the private sector as these activities are transferred from BR ownership.

---

[1] See *Gaining Access to the Railway Network* (DoT, 1993, para. 5.1).

The Government's rôle has already been mentioned in connection with each player. Government will set objectives and budgets for each of them. It can pay subsidy under several different headings. It can also intervene directly, as it does with the present nationalised industries.

However, several production activities which are currently subject to government objectives by virtue of being within British Railways, will escape from them: for instance, franchised train operations, vehicle leasing, and track engineering.

4. Railway Economics[1]

THE FRANCHISING DIRECTOR has to make decisions on what changes to make to a service or a set of services. RailTrack, with the approval of the Regulator for the general principles, must select charges for the use of infrastructure, including charges to be levied on those who exercise rights of open access. Thus, the new decision-makers will have to be aware of cost conditions and requirements for efficient pricing. A considerable amount of information and analysis will be required. Some of the problems are discussed below.

Avoidable Costs

A central question is what effect a change will have on total system cost (the avoidable cost of the change). As *Gaining Access...* notes, if a charge for a service is less than the avoidable costs, then system revenues net of system costs will be greater if the service were removed. If the charge is greater than the avoidable costs, then the service is making a positive net contribution towards covering other system costs.

Common Costs

The Franchising Director may consider putting on one service. That would incur its avoidable cost. He may consider putting on a different service, so incurring a different avoidable cost. He might consider putting on both as part of a package which would have its own avoidable cost which would typically be less than the sum of the two

---

[1.] Much of the relevant technical material is touched upon in *Gaining Access...* (DoT, 1993).

individual avoidable costs. The reason is that there may be *common* or *joint* costs.[1]

The problem of joint and common costs causes considerable debate in railways. Accountants often exhaust all costs by allocating them to one activity or another. But accounting costs are of limited guidance in setting charges. From an economic point of view there is no sense in attempting to allocate common costs to anything in particular. By definition, the act of allocating them can only be misleading and cannot provide any useful guidance on any decision.

Inevitably, the proportion of costs which has to be classified as common increases as activities are disaggregated.[2] At the other end of the scale, there are no common costs in the railway taken as a whole: all of the costs of the railway are avoidable by closing it. The problems of common costs will therefore be emphasised if the Franchising Director breaks down the activities to be franchised into small 'lots'. In the definition of avoidable costs and common costs, the *relevant* costs are not absolute but are tied to the particular decision at issue.

Efficient Pricing

At several points we shall refer to the notion of 'efficient prices'. This is a precisely defined term in economics, though its implications depend considerably on the context.[3]

When a commodity is freely traded, the price paid will represent the benefit to the purchaser of one extra unit (the 'marginal' unit). If the price is equal to the total social costs of providing the extra unit, then it is said to be efficient. If a price is not efficient, then the benefit in consumption is different from the cost of supply and there is scope for improving the situation for everybody by changing the quantity traded. On the other hand, if a price is efficient, then any change which makes some individual better off must necessarily be at the expense of some other individual's welfare.

Inefficient prices are economically wasteful: hence the interest in attempting to set efficient prices. However, an efficient price relates to the total social cost of the extra unit, including not only rail costs but

---

[1] These principles are set out in more detail in Beesley and Kettle (1985).
[2] Beesley and Kettle (1985), *op. cit.,* p.14.
[3] See, for example, Glaister (1987).

[25]

also an imputation for any such items as pollution and congestion costs ('externalities') imposed on those other than its consumers. The combination of common costs in railways and the presence of externalities creates complexity in judging efficiency in pricing.

Models of Cost and Revenue Causation

Published evidence on the nature of railway costs shows some consensus.[1] It seems that there are approximately constant returns to scale (as network size is varied) beyond a minimum efficient firm size. There are clear economies of traffic density, largely attributable to improved deployment of staff and vehicles, the ability to mount longer trains, thus using track capacity more efficiently, and better node interconnection. However, the evidence is dominated by US experience with many private railway companies. It is not clear to what extent this freight-based experience in US geographical conditions can be transferred to the UK. Much research needs to be done to bring our knowledge of the UK up to a usable standard. Economies of scale and of density are quite different from economies of scope, which are the savings which accrue to running different services on one system. It is the latter which give rise to the joint or common costs noted above.

In practice, there are some situations in Britain's railways where there is a shortage of track capacity: extra trains can be run only by either spending money on improving physical assets or delaying other trains. If there is a shortage of track capacity it is necessary to distinguish short-run marginal costs from medium-run marginal costs after investment in signalling has been made to stretch capacity, and then true long-run marginal costs after the whole infrastructure has been expanded. It is said that doubling up track less than doubles costs and more than quadruples capacity.[2] That may be so in rural areas but, as with roads, it seems less likely to be the case in built-up areas where the costs of new land take are high, quite apart from the public opposition that probably renders increasing land take for railways impractical in the UK in most situations. Thus long-run marginal capacity costs are high, with the consequence that efficient track

---

[1] See Nash and Preston (1992), Dodgson (1993?), and Friedlaender *et al.* (1993).
[2] See Nash and Preston (1992), *op. cit.*

[26]

pricing may yield substantial rents (profits) to the owners of the existing infrastructure.

Economies of density may imply higher unit charges on sparse parts of the network than on densely used parts. Even so, costs may not be fully covered in such situations because of the nature of the cost structure (declining average costs in part due to fixed costs).

Knowledge is imperfect about relationships among track costs and train speeds, train axle weights, suspension design, and other factors. Engineers have had information on these factors for some time, but there has been little visible evidence of their application in the economics of rail operations, charging or accounting in the UK to date. Stewart Joy (1973) showed that progress was possible on these topics. There may be a 'power law' relating axle weights to damage costs analogous to the well-established power laws for highways, with all that implies for efficient charging and maintenance strategies.

A sophisticated understanding of the industry's cost structure will be required, including cost causation in infrastructure maintenance and investment, cost causation in train and terminal operations, and the way in which services interact in congested circumstances given the track configurations relevant to particular services. All these issues will have to be brought together in costing and pricing train paths. British Rail has some expertise in modelling these issues which will have to be preserved. Both the Regulator and the Franchising Director will require access to this information and the ability to operate the models for their own purposes. They, and RailTrack, will also have new requirements. Existing models are inevitably imperfect, not least because they were designed for different purposes; they will have to be developed to meet the requirements of the new structure.

Cost Recovery

If a service or group of services is charged at least its system avoidable costs, the finances of the system are better off with it than without any services at all. Conversely, it would not be sensible to close a service or group of services that could cover its avoidable costs.

It is unlikely that congestion will be a problem on much of the British Rail network. But there are some congested places, such as the approaches to London, where the cost of expanding capacity

[27]

sufficiently cannot be justified. In congested parts of the network, introducing a new service would impose costs on other services and system-avoidable costs would be above those directly associated with the service. It will be possible, and probably desirable, for RailTrack to charge rates which will extract some or all of the rents deriving from the ownership of assets which would enjoy excess demand at cost-based prices - essentially congestion charges.[1]

One issue is to what extent profits from high-demand franchises can be appropriated to make the efficient pricing of low-demand sites sustainable and thereby keep open some services which would otherwise close. Before this even becomes a possibility, an argument will have to be won to establish the principle that rents earned on profitable franchises, which technically would have to be paid directly to the Exchequer, will be made available as a net increase in the Franchising Director's budget. This increase can be achieved by taking the anticipated rents into account in advance in the process of setting the budget, in time exposing the magnitude of the gross subsidy. Another difficult issue is how charges can be set which give sensible signals to RailTrack as to what capacity and speed standards to maintain, which track to keep open, where to propose closure; and which will allow the break-even and other objectives to be met over the long term.

If impartial principles can be set, they will establish a proper commercial basis which will help to limit the direct intervention by government which tends to accompany continuing membership of the public sector. The problem is interactive, depending on predicting values and costs in a highly contingent manner, so it is especially important that the parties are left to negotiate and exchange information without interference.

Difficulties in Practice

One practical problem is whether it will be accepted that, while a metre of rail track in North Wales may look the same as a metre of track on an approach to London, they are different economic commodities which can carry different charges for their use. Some

---

[1.] This is assuming that these rents are not given away to operators through the granting of 'grandfather rights', as has happened to some airlines at some airports.

debates about the 'fairness' of urban road pricing suggest this will not be a trivial matter.

In endorsing the principle of relating infrastructure charges to avoidable costs, *Gaining Access...* presents two problems, although it does not acknowledge them explicitly. *First*, it says that

> 'Work carried out . . . has confirmed that the majority of rail infrastructure costs are common, that is, they cannot be uniquely attributed to any particular operator or even class of operator. The majority of costs also tend to be fixed, at least in the short to medium term' (DoT, 1993, para.3.2).

If that is correct then, whilst the principle of avoidable cost-based charging is a useful starting point, it will give little help to RailTrack or the Regulator in covering the majority of costs. It will leave a large unallocated 'rump' of costs whose allocation could generate distorting signals.[1]

The *second* problem is that, apart from the end of the sentence from *Gaining Access...* quoted in the paragraph above, there is no mention of the time-scale to be considered. There is often a fundamental difference between immediately avoidable costs and those that can be avoided over a period long enough to entail an adjustment to the capital investment programme. If capital investment is smoothly variable and if it is at its optimal level, there is no distinction between long-run avoidable and short-run avoidable costs. But railways fulfil neither of these conditions; thus there will be many situations where attempting to cover long-run avoidable costs would lead to a different outcome from covering short-run avoidable costs. A well-known example occurs where long-lived infrastructure – a viaduct, say – can continue for a period before expensive maintenance work will be required. Mindless application of a long-run cost notion, or of accounting costs in such a situation could lead to premature closure.

By the same token, failure to include a proper charge for the

---

[1] This conclusion is at odds with the evidence presented by Beesley and Kettle (1985) in the context of the railway in Victoria, Australia: they estimated that only about 20 per cent of system total costs were common. Permanent way, signalling and administration and technical services accounted for over half of these joint costs. They found that only 30 per cent of 'commonality' in track and signalling is technical – the rest is by choice, for economic convenience.

renewal of long-lived infrastructure can overstate the true contribution made by a service. Many railway assets have physical lives of the order of 30 to 50 years, with gently declining quality of performance if not fully maintained. So the decision must be made *ab initio* either to run a service for a limited period before closure and ignore the long-run costs of infrastructure renewal – which would be irrelevant – or to run it in perpetuity and make a full charge for long-term infrastructure maintenance.

Gaining Access... recognises some implications of its view of the technological characteristics of the system. The main one is that it will be necessary to adopt a strategy of 'market pricing' (para.3.4), that is, charging what the market will bear. Those train paths able to make a greater contribution to total costs will be required to do so. Estimating which these services are will, of course, be difficult. It will require an understanding of the demand for rail services, and therefore access to the demand models which British Rail has developed, in parallel with the access to the cost models discussed above. Ownership of these models will be critical. The document also notes that it will be necessary to avoid 'unfair' discrimination between competing operators *in the same market*. These words are not straightforward to interpret and it will be a major function of the Regulator to provide an interpretation within the bounds of competition law.

There are some major issues to be resolved concerning the way RailTrack is to operate. Some are straightforward in principle, though contentious in practice, such as what rate of return is to be earned by RailTrack on its assets, and what asset base is to be used. Other issues are much harder. The objective will be a break-even constraint, after some capital grants and after deducting a return on the assets. As long as RailTrack remains in the public sector (unlike the National Grid in electricity) there will be potential conflicts between the 'usual controls exercised over nationalised industries' (as they will apply to a Government-owned company) mentioned in the White Paper and the Regulator's wishes. In the past Ministers have shown themselves eager to intervene in matters that British Rail and London Transport regarded as within their own competence. There would be temptation to do so again in the case of RailTrack – for instance, in pricing the use of particular pieces of track that affect some local interest.

Furthermore, the Government has not stated what is to happen if it turns out that, over the last few years, track investment has been insufficient to maintain the state of the track at its present size. For instance, there may have been significant under-investment in maintenance of track bed and structures (especially bridges) - hence the argument that British Rail should have been put in 'good shape' over a period of years before the attempt to privatise. If so, how is this catching up to be financed? If too heavy a burden is placed on the operating revenues of the railway, innovations in services that would be worthwhile in the long run (because they could cover their long-run attributable cost) could be stillborn because they could not sustain the cost of making good historic under-investment. Unlike some other privatised industries, there is not enough potential profit in railways to make good such under-investment. The outcome might be a requirement for subsidy, though there would be operating efficiency gains to set against such a subsidy. Discussions about catching up on past under-investment (or not doing so) will have political overtones and could result in interference with the independence of the new rail industry actors.

Information

At present the British Railways Board, in principle at least, has full and free access to all management information. In the proposed system the Regulator and, in particular, the Franchising Director will have to obtain this information from separate organisations - RailTrack, British Rail and independent operators. They will need to know what to ask for and who to ask, and they will have to recognise that there will be incentives to hide or distort information.[1]

We have already discussed the central importance of the various models which exist for estimating costs and the importance of developing them. Later, we make similar comments on revenue

---

[1] Bös (1993) points out that this is recognised as a general problem in the theory of privatisation as the structure of a principal-agent problem changes. The principal is further distanced from the agents which may imply an increase in the costs of securing what the principal desires. Therefore the principal will settle for less achievement. Against this, it is said that in any case the present incentive structure is such that the Board does not husband or use its information adequately.

[31]

models (below, p.53). It is not simply a matter of giving the regulatory authorities access to information in the sense of facts and figures. What is crucial is an understanding of the underlying physical and economic relationships which explain, in quantitative terms, how changes in some things affect other things. These relationships are embodied in large, computer-based models, owned and run by BR, embodying various assumptions and with documentation of variable quality. Gaining effective access to these models requires that they be operated by co-operative individuals who know them intimately. Existing models will have to be kept up to date as new information is generated. They will also require development as understanding of the fundamentals of railway economics improves. Maintaining the quality of BR's existing models and ensuring future access - perhaps via a common, impartial source of expertise - will be an essential element in the success (or failure) of privatisation.

5. Controls, Subsidy and Incentives

Controls

THE PURISTIC APPROACH to privatising an industry would be to find a way in which the new industrial structure, products, prices and qualities could emerge as a result of the operation of 'market forces'. The rail privatisation proposals, however, appear carefully designed to constrain change in order to make the policy workable in practical and political terms. This is illustrated in the quotations reproduced in Box 1 (below, pp.34-35).

Gaining Access... reveals that, in effect, RailTrack will eventually take the lead on service planning, with the Franchising Director following this lead (see the quotations reproduced in Box 2, below, pp.36-37). Taken together, the statements in the boxes imply that RailTrack will be firmly in the lead in determining the long-term direction of the industry. This notion appears to have developed since the publication of the White Paper, which gave an impression that the Franchising Director would be sitting in the middle of the web, essentially using a large budget to buy the use of track infrastructure from a compliant supplier, and selling it on to his agent-operators at a

[32]

discount. However, RailTrack will, in time, become the main principal with the Franchising Director acting as a wholesaling agent.

The quotations also make it clear that the Government will have control over all aspects of the activities of the Franchising Authority, and of RailTrack so long as it remains in the public sector. The Franchising Authority will have to agree its programme of activities with the Government. The Government will set 'broad objectives for service levels, service quality and fares', and the Franchising Director and RailTrack will work within government constraints.

In his Second Reading speech on the Railways Bill, the Secretary of State for Transport stated his intention that RailTrack should act as a 'truly independent, commercially driven body'. But the fact is that if the Government (in its many departmental guises) does not like the activities of the Franchising Authority or RailTrack, there will be opportunities for intervention. The best that can be said for all this proposed governmental oversight and control is that it may make more explicit the political nature of railways. Nonetheless, it is not 'privatisation' in the sense that this term has been used for other British denationalisation schemes.

The Many Routes for Subsidy

As *Gaining Access...* notes, 'The Franchising Director and Railtrack will work within constraints set by Government' (para.6.5). The same will be true of residual British Rail operations. Thus the Government has preserved firm control of these players, through the purse strings as well as in the other ways that we have noted. So long as the Franchising Director and RailTrack work within financing limits set by the Government, the discretionary funding of the whole railway – including train services, investment and maintenance – will remain within a system which is controlled by the Treasury's year-to-year funding decisions. In water, gas, electricity and British Telecom, privatisation means total financial freedom (apart from the activities of the independent regulators) for the new privatised industries. But for railways there will be no possibility of long-term security of funding for the industry so long as it remains within the public spending system. Only the Regulator does not have to worry about the size of future grants – except, of course, in the context of the budget for his own office which will remain in the gift of government.

There is an important difference from the present situation, in that the Railways Board currently uses internal cross-subsidy so that profitable activities help to fund the unprofitable, and the *net* subsidy appears in the public accounts. The total subsidy will thus become transparent and subject to explicit parliamentary approval. The subsidy will also, other things being equal, appear to rise at the start of the new system.

In the immediate future, since the railway will continue to function, a large subsidy will continue to be given to British Rail. In the long term the intention is that most of the subsidy should pass through the hands of the Franchising Director, with an increasing proportion used for franchised services and a diminishing proportion for 'block' PSO grant. How much goes on direct support to services which the

[34]

Network, DoT Consultation Document, 1993, para.4.2.)

'Competition from other operators to use the same route will be moderated to the extent necessary to ensure the successful launch of the first generation of franchises. And some access rights will be 'grandfathered' under contracts with other operators, for example existing contracts between British Rail and freight operators, and certain international services.' (*Gaining Access...*, para.5.2.)

'The starting point for splitting capacity will be the timetable for 1994. For freight services, the starting point will be the requirements fixed by existing contracts with British Rail which remain in force after Railtrack is established. ...Railtrack will...be responsible for adjusting the split between passenger and freight paths in the light of market demand, subject to the constraints imposed by existing access agreements and consistent with it meeting the financial targets set by Government.' (*Gaining Access...*, para.3.9.)

'The Government will determine the broad programme of franchising which will be implemented by the Franchising Director.' (*Gaining Access...*, para.6.4.)

'The Franchising Director and Railtrack will work within constraints set by Government.' (*Gaining Access...*, para.6.5.)

Government has decided not to close depends upon the number of closure proposals coming forward from the Franchising Director and accepted by the Regulator. It also depends upon the Government's willingness to allow closures. In the past all governments have found rail closures difficult to sanction. Several different government departments, notably those in Wales and Scotland, will be involved.

Until the rail privatisation policy has had time to produce genuine productivity improvements in the industry, *and* any backlog of investment has been made good *and* future investment requirements are properly funded, it will only be possible to reduce state support at the price of a contraction in the size of the system, reduction in service frequency, run-down of the condition of the assets or raising revenues through fares increases in the situations (like London commuting) where that may be profitable. Otherwise funding shortfalls would be concentrated in visible and embarrassing situations and the consequences would be wrongly blamed on the rail privatisation policy itself. It is difficult to know how the Government can credibly promise that levels of funding will be maintained meanwhile, particularly in view of the current public expenditure climate. But, in order to give the policy a fair chance of success, it probably needs to do so.

Justifications for Subsidy

The Government is creating several separate justifications for subsidy:

- capital grants to RailTrack;
- the Franchising Director's budget for franchised passenger services;
- PSO grant to the residual British Rail services;
- payments to prevent closure of specified services;
- subsidies paid by local authorities.

As is normal, the Bill refers to 'the Secretary of State' without to improve efficiency and ensure that the allocation of access rights is market determined.'

'There will be little difference for operators between this approach and that adopted for the first generation of franchises. They will however have more flexibility as to which groups of services they choose to bid for.' (*Gaining Access...*, paras. 6.15-6.18.)

'When changes to the timetable affect more than one operator, they are best discussed and agreed multilaterally, rather than through a series of bilateral negotiations. Railtrack will be expected to have regular discussions with operators, of which the most formal expression is likely to be timetabling conferences which might also involve the Franchising Director. Given the pivotal rôle of the timetabling process in the allocation of access, the Regulator is likely to take an interest in such conferences.' (*Gaining Access...*, para. 7.9.)

specifying which one. The Act would therefore give powers to *any* Secretary of State. In particular, the Secretaries of State for Scotland and Wales would have independent powers to give subsidies to prevent rail closures. The firm intention is that in due course all subsidies will, formally speaking, pass through the Franchising Director's budget. But they will inevitably be 'ring-fenced' to a substantial degree. That is, the Franchising Director will have limited discretion to transfer money given for one purpose to some other of his choosing. At the same time, the Franchising Director will become accountable for these monies, which will greatly expand his responsibilities beyond those for the budget for his own franchised services.

Yet one more justification for subsidy appeared for the first time in a statement to Parliament and spelt out in *Gaining Access...* (para.4.6). Under the 'New Track Charge Grant Scheme' for freight operators,

'revenue grant of up to 100% of the charge negotiated with Railtrack would be available, where this was necessary to retain or attract traffic to rail and justified in terms of the wider benefits obtained'.

This scheme will operate within a fixed budget - although no indication has yet been given of the total size of this budget. If the Roads Programme is a precedent, two other routes for subsidy will be via the Welsh Office and the Scottish Office which each have their own budgets and criteria for supporting their infrastructures.

How will different government departments view this complexity? Some may welcome it because it provides much scope to adapt to changing and unforeseen circumstances. The channels will be available to nip blossoming political awkwardness in the bud. By the same token, it is hard to believe that those responsible for public expenditure control - particularly the Treasury - will approve: the system creates a bewildering number of dykes into which fingers will have to be put. Subsidy would be simpler to understand and easier to control if it were put into the hands of the Franchising Director as a lump sum, in the same way as it now passes through the hands of the British Railways Board, which can be treated as a single entity for public expenditure control purposes.

Incentives

The subsidy system creates some incentives that may not have been intended. If the Franchising Director calculates that the Government will step in to save services that are recommended for closure, then the closure procedure will be seen as a way of forcing the Government to fund services for which there is insufficient budget provision. Rural services in politically marginal areas will be particularly susceptible to such incentives.

At present there is substantial cross-subsidy between services within each of the British Rail sectors. RailTrack preserves the ability to look across the whole system. However, there will now be a further complication to an already complicated problem: the Franchising Director has the ability (and the incentives) to bundle services in ways that suit his purposes. If the Franchising Director sells a particular set of services for a positive bid, the funds must be returned to the Exchequer. If he sells one for a negative bid it will count against his budget. So, to make his budget produce as much railway service as possible, the Franchising Director has an incentive to bundle profitable

[38]

services with the unprofitable. That way as few bundles as possible will be sold at a positive price.

6. Issues

Labour Market Competition

CAPITAL RECEIPTS from asset sales are likely to be small, but a major benefit the policy could offer over a period of years is a reduction in the annual state subsidy to the railway – or an increase in rail services for the same subsidy. Privatisation is more likely to achieve this result by reducing labour costs than by stimulating demand which is dominated by the state of the national economy.

British Rail has made considerable gains in labour productivity over recent years, even though it has not had the benefit that experience in the bus market suggests could be available through competition in the labour market. However, the White Paper gives no estimate of what further productivity gains may be expected from privatisation, so it is not possible to make an informed judgement on how much more efficient in its use of labour the industry might become. The 1984 White Paper on bus policy[1] did publish an estimate of what was anticipated and that formed a powerful argument in support of the legislation. Likely productivity increases are so important a pillar in support of the new railways policy that it would be helpful if the Government were to publish an approximate estimate.

Although a great deal of public attention is focussed on changes in services and their providers, a significant part of the real action will be in the markets for the supply of factors, especially labour. A vital task is to establish firmly and from the beginning that the procedures must not be designed in a way that will inhibit proper competition in the labour market. For instance, the imposition of standards on franchised operators in respect of whom they employ and on what terms (beyond the normal employment legislation, requirements of EC legislation and safety requirements) may forestall an opportunity for a major unit cost reduction in the industry.

Organised labour will lobby against this principle. But it is not entirely against employees' own interests. If the kind of unit cost

1.*Buses*, DoT, Cmnd.9300, London: HMSO, 1984.

reduction that bus deregulation has achieved (as was predicted) can be obtained in the rail industry, and if state support does not contract £-for-£, then employment may increase with increased output. Or at least it may not decline as fast as it has been doing without privatisation. Moreover, there is greater job satisfaction in working in an enterprise that is doing well.

The fact that 70 per cent of British Rail drivers will retire by the year 2000 may appear to be unfortunate because of new training costs, but it means that changes of attitude can occur through the natural process of replacement. For instance, if the new, young staff are recruited by independent companies, it is not certain that they will choose to join the established national rail unions, or any union at all.

Private Investment in Infrastructure and Train Operations

The Regulator and Franchising Director will give attention to providing the kinds of opportunities that will attract those with funds to invest. That will entail creating appropriate risk and return patterns, appropriate term structures of debt, and generally enabling investors to create portfolios so as to manage their risks. Attracting investors will require clarity about the regulatory rules of the game and the greatest possible reassurance that future governments will not give way to popular pressure in ways that will compromise investments. It will involve responding positively to the investors' own proposals: they will think of new ways of bundling economic activities to create attractive investments. For instance, they may wish to invest in complete transport corridors, exploiting complementary activities like property, the local road system, and park-and-ride. Such schemes might well involve partnership with local authorities, Development Agencies and even government departments.

Here the potential contribution of local authorities should be considered. They are already significant funders of rail services with British Rail acting as their agents. They will be able to continue in this capacity, with the Franchising Director letting franchises on their behalf. Privatisation will produce many new ways that local authorities could become involved. For instance, there is international bond finance looking for a 'home' which might include railway assets. Local authorities could act as guarantors and intermediaries to channel that finance into track and rolling stock assets for local use, although some relaxation of Treasury rules may be necessary.

Open Access

It is proposed that eventually any (licensed) operator who wishes will have equal access to the rail infrastructure.[1] This is consistent with the current policy of the European Commission in respect of specified types of international services. The objective is to create competition on the tracks. In principle, the outcome could be that passenger services on profitable routes would be provided entirely by 'open access' operators in competition with one another. Services on unprofitable routes would be operated under franchises, if the Franchising Director decided they were worth running at all. There would be a middle ground – possibly most of the services – where franchises would be operated but they would be at risk from an open-access competitor.

Open access has advantages, but permitting it makes for complications. It will expose the holder of a franchise to the commercial risk from an open-access competitor, especially in those cases where the service in question is sufficiently commercially attractive for the franchise to carry a positive price. It will mean that the Franchise Director must arrange to share out infrastructure capacity as and when required, rather than designing for the more predictable needs of defined contracts of a predetermined length.

Most importantly, open access implies that competition will eliminate most of the profits currently used to cross-subsidise loss-making services. Nobody will be willing to pay a high positive price for a revenue-risk-bearing franchise to operate a service if competitive entry is likely from open-access providers. If such competition occurs, the beneficiaries will be the users of services that currently make profits: they will benefit from service improvements and lower fares. The losers will be general taxpayers, who must make good the lost cross-subsidies to the extent that loss-making services are preserved.

Giving equal access to tracks for operators from other European countries will be more attractive if it can be shown that all member-

---

[1.] As we have noted above, this policy has been moderated for the letting of the first franchises.

countries are doing the same – rather than just saying they are going to do it but putting obstacles in the way. The UK stands to gain from this policy because it has efficient rail operators by European standards and because it seems likely that the fashion for rail-building in Europe will create more new opportunities outside the UK than in it. However, the difficulties with tax harmonisation for goods vehicles and other transport liberalisation policies, together with strongly expressed opposition to free access from non-UK rail operators and organisations, are worrying. Pressure may have to be applied to ensure consistency of accounting conventions, the avoidance of hidden subsidies, and the erection of administrative impediments to equal access.

The Role of Profit

The title 'Regulator' has a negative and inappropriate connotation in railways. With earlier UK privatisations the industry in question was virtually guaranteed a growing future in which profitable opportunities would be created. It was equally obvious that the 'public interest' had to be protected by the restraining force of regulation because market power existed and markets were not being made fully competitive. When they were nationalised monopolies, these industries would have been able to exploit their monopoly power to the detriment of consumers had they had complete freedom.

Railways are different in that there are few opportunities for profit, and long-term growth is not assured. British Rail has a *monopoly* of rail services but much of it has little monopoly *power* because of competition from alternative modes of transport. It is presently more free of *any* kind of economic regulation than are private companies: the normal strictures of fair trading and competition law are not applied. Much of the railway is highly commercial in its attitudes. Hence the plethora of different fares charged, emulating airline pricing structures.

The rail Regulator will presumably be conscious of the danger of imposing new restrictions in a way that would stifle the delicate prospects for the industry. The job will be more positive than the repressive term 'regulator' implies. In partnership with the Franchising Director and RailTrack, the task will be predominantly one of fostering new markets and creating the conditions under which they can flourish. Among other things, this will involve creating

[42]

circumstances in which it will be sensible for investors to take risks, thereby developing markets through the normal evolutionary process of trial and error.

At a minimum, private sector interests must earn 'normal profits' – a return sufficient to keep them in the industry and prevent them from diverting their efforts to some other. Only if they can expect to make profits will investors take risks and offset the inevitable losses associated with innovations, some of which will inevitably fail. Profit must come to be seen as the just reward for providing what users want at prices they are prepared to pay, in railways as in most other commodities. There is so little monopoly power in many rail *operating* markets (excluding London commuter services and some others) that the Regulator will find little justification for intervention if a rail operator is clever enough to make profits. Because of the auctioning process, profits higher than normal profits will be predominantly achieved as a consequence of gains in efficiency on the cost side.

For franchised services, franchises must be renewed by the Franchising Director under a competitive process sufficiently often that opportunities for excess profit are competed away and the state abstracts the excess profits for profitable services, or pays the minimum possible subsidy for the loss-makers. The nature of the contracts must be such as to preclude the earning of unjustified profits by subsequent renegotiations such as special pleading about unanticipated inflation or other costs: risks must be shared sensibly.

The real case for competition is that it is about creating variety, testing markets, trying out new ways of doing things and moving the companies in question in the direction of doing well what they do best. Conversely, it is about withdrawing from activities they are not able to do particularly well. Competition is not simply about driving everybody's costs to the bare bone. Yet the rail privatisation proposals will initially accept the present broad pattern of activities and apply pressure to reduce their costs. Over a period of time the Franchising Director may be able to devise ways of testing the market by allowing patterns of bundling services to emerge in the bidding process.

Competition and Fair-Trading Legislation

Currently, the railways are exempt from the provisions of the competition and fair-trading legislation that apply to most goods and services, as was the bus industry before the 1985 Act that deregulated it. The implications of weakening this exemption could be extensive - although they are not easy to predict as experience with the bus industry illustrates. There may be many situations in which the choice is between having no rail services at all or exploiting such opportunities as there are for price discrimination and forming restrictive agreements with other transport operators.

The issue is likely to be particularly acute in freight services. British Rail has been allowed to negotiate freight rates privately with each individual customer, without publishing tariffs. Its commercial remit will have led it to extract the maximum it can from each customer rather than relating charges in some way to the costs of carrying the particular traffic. Despite this, and even though it is generously treated in the present system of prime-user costing, the freight business is making substantial losses (above, page 15). Yet the Government proposes to sell the freight businesses outright. Any attempt to restrict freight's ability to practice price discrimination will enlarge the section of the business which is uneconomic and which will have to be abandoned in order to make sale of the companies possible.

As with other privatisation legislation, the Railways Bill makes provision for the Restrictive Trades Practices Act to be disapplied in an order made by the Secretary of State, though it is not at present clear which kinds of agreement will be affected. The Bill also makes provision for the Regulator to share the powers of the Director General of Fair Trading in respect of railway services, so that the two will consult each other and thus avoid duplication. The Director General will be able to delegate his responsibilities to the Regulator, who will be able to exercise the powers in his general policies, thus reducing the risk of repeating the confusion over policies and principles which has arisen in the bus industry.

Avoiding Litigation

The Regulator and Franchising Director will have to deal on several different dimensions with each of more than 18 different kinds of bodies: safety authorities, RailTrack, British Rail operations, franchisees, private sector operators not operating franchises, rolling-stock owners and maintainers, the Department of Transport, the Treasury, the Department of Trade, the Welsh and Scottish Offices, fair trading and competition authorities, the EC, users' committees, unions, local authorities, investors, and each other. Quite apart from the potential cost and obstruction that an overly formal and litigious approach risks, it is doubtful whether it would be feasible to tie up all the loose ends in a consistent way. It is therefore imperative to achieve as much as possible by common consent, while recognising that disputes will inevitably arise which will have to be determined by the Regulator. There will be a large premium on forms of contract that are incentive-compatible and self-enforcing.

In the Consultation Document on railway franchising (DoT, 1992b), it is envisaged that the agreed contract will allow the franchisee to vary the normal terms 'in the event that the demand for passenger services declines by more than a specified amount during the franchise period for specified *reasons outside the franchisee's control*' (our italics). This kind of provision is presumably intended to reduce the commercial risks. But it is a potential source of litigation because of the necessity to establish what was and what was not a result of the franchisee's actions. For example, how much of a fall in demand was due to the franchisee raising fares? The whole issue of efficient risk-bearing, and the corresponding contract structure, will require careful analysis by the Franchise Director in consultation with the Regulator, who has to approve the form of the contracts.

The Licensing Function

One function identified for the Regulator is the 'validation' and licensing of operators, a rôle fulfilled by the Traffic Commissioners for the commercial vehicle and bus industries. The restrictions imposed in the 1930s on the back of safety licensing may not have mattered much when the bus industry was highly profitable and essentially well adjusted to its markets. But they came to matter much more after the 1950s when decline set in and markets moved. The electricity regulation legislation seems to have established a set of criteria for suitability as a generator which can be expected to impede competitive entry as little as possible. The rail Regulator will have to do the same.

No mention is made of the mechanisms envisaged to provide a right of appeal against decisions not to issue licences to particular operators. The experience of bus and road haulage licensing shows clearly that an appeal mechanism is necessary. If it works well then it helps the system enormously: natural justice is not denied and yet the authority of the licensor is enhanced if occasional appeals against his decisions are not upheld. The Transport Tribunal seems to have been successful in this way in the bus and road haulage industries under the 1985 Act.

An Operator of Last Resort

Occasional company failure is an unavoidable feature of successful competition for contracts: attempts to guarantee that it will not happen can only lead back to state-run, non-competitive industry. The prospect of failure of private sector operators raises the issue of security of supply of a public service. In the bus industry, sufficient operators have assets that can be redeployed flexibly, so that an authority can replace a missing service at short notice.

The Railways Bill makes specific provision for putting administrators into a failing operator to allow the staff and the assets to continue to function until alternative arrangements can be made. London bus tendering has shown that having an alternative 'operator of last resort' is useful even if company failure is not an immediate prospect. It would give the Franchising Director the credible threat that he can and will terminate a contract if there is good reason to do so. It would be useful for other reasons. It is a means of providing public service continuity in the event that contractors have their contracts terminated for non-performance (which will happen). It would also be a comfort while auctioning franchises because, in essence, it provides a reserve position against the possibility that all private sector bids are unreasonably high, either through lack of effective competition for a particular contract, because of collusion amongst bidders or simply because of inexperience and error by all bidders. As a corollary, it gives the Franchising Director more freedom to be adventurous.

It seems, therefore, that British Rail operations will have a rôle to play, at the very least until the franchising market is well established with a large number of reliable players. This may limit the rate at which British Rail operations should be run down, although there is a danger that if British Rail comes to be seen as a second division operator whose main function is to step in and clear up after somebody else's failure it will damage management morale. One possibility would be that British Rail should be allowed to bid in the first place in its own right, on the London Bus model. So far this has been ruled out: one advantage of preventing it is that the residual 'block grant' to BR would be isolated and any leakage into bids for franchises would be blocked. In any case, bidding by BR would not be compatible with the notion that British Rail is to be phased out quickly.

The Consultation Document on franchising suggests that bids from independent operators will not be accepted if none of the bids received is judged to represent adequate value for money, in which case British Rail will continue to operate the relevant services for the time being. One difficulty is that this implies that the Franchising Director has a thorough understanding of the relevant British Rail costs and so can judge whether or not value for money means leaving the operation with them. In practice, such judgements will be difficult. An advantage of allowing the incumbent operator to bid is that the Franchising Director need only be concerned with the bid and not with the basis on which it is constructed. Over time the bids will reveal information about costs. There would, however, be a need for an audit mechanism to ensure that British Rail's bids were constructed according to specified criteria.

The Market for Rolling Stock

A properly functioning market for rolling stock is a necessary condition for the success of the franchising system. So there is another set of markets to be nurtured. There should be no fundamental difficulty in doing so, given the vast experience of the variety of arrangements which flourish in other transport industries - notably aviation, where the life of the main assets is of the same order as that of trains. There may be benefits in integrating the functions of asset ownership and asset maintenance so that the owner has the correct incentives to maintain his assets to maximise their whole-life value. If he is also the manufacturer he may have a comparative advantage in maintenance techniques.

However, railways have special features. Maintenance facilities are geographically specific. For historical reasons, power supply and signalling systems are not standardised which, along with other factors, limits the transferability of rolling stock between lines. Thus situations of bilateral monopoly will be created between stock owners and operators. The Regulator may have to arbitrate in cases where negotiations fail to produce a sensible outcome. Where stock can be transferred between lines – as on some of the Network SouthEast system – the second-hand and lease markets must run smoothly to match the flexibility rail managers now have to move stock around the system. Responsive markets will have the advantage of clearly reacting to incentives to use stock in the most efficient ways. In other situations rolling stock will be tied to a specific set of lines. The Franchising Director may wish to own the rolling stock – or to create a separate body to own it – and let franchises with the rolling stock supplied as part of the contract.

As Jones *et al.* (1993) point out, choice of the length of franchise contract is a matter of balancing the necessity to maintain competitive pressure on the local monopolies which will be created, against the desire of bidders to spread the ownership costs of their assets over the longest possible contract. Reducing the ownership risks tips the balance in favour of more frequent competitions for the franchises. Five years is a long time to hold a monopoly: it is undesirable to let contracts for longer if it can be avoided.

The Form of the Franchise Bidding

Bidding for franchises is likely to be by sealed bid, first-price bidding on the amount to be paid for the right to operate a service or services to a specification declared in advance by the Franchising Director. Bidders will make assessments of the fares they will be able to charge passengers. The bids will depend on the limits declared by the Regulator (in the case of services regarded as in need of price control because of significant monopoly power) and (in other cases) on bidders' views about the likely competitive market conditions.

Another form of auction would be of the Chadwick-Demsetz variety,[1] where the level of subsidy (positive or negative) would be

[1] See Antony W. Dnes, *On the Wrong Tracks: The Government's Proposals for Franchising Passenger Rail,* Hume Occasional Paper No.40, Edinburgh: The David Hume Institute, 1993.

declared and bidders would bid on the fares they would charge to passengers. This can be a good way to franchise profitable natural monopolies in that it extracts any producer rents for the benefit of consumers and gives them the lowest prices, together with productive efficiency.

However, we doubt whether this would be an appropriate or workable procedure in this case. *First*, whilst productive efficiency is certainly an objective, it is not self-evident that the aim should be to yield the lowest possible fares for passengers and leave no rents with producers or the owners of the right to produce (that is, with the state). There is a conflict which has been present in other privatisations: creating fierce (price) competition in the privatised industry reduces the industry's sale value. Conversely, limiting competition captures some value for the taxpayer at the expense of the consumer. In the past the Government has chosen to retain some of the potential value as a contribution to the Exchequer, even though this has been at the expense of the ultimate economic efficiency of the industry. Arguably, a similar strategy is legitimate in the case of the railways, with the state seeking, in the long run, to redress the balance in favour of the taxpayers (who currently contribute over £1 billion a year).

Second, there is the practical problem that parts of the industry are in areas of significant monopoly power, having price elasticities much less than unity. In these circumstances, it is not obvious that bidding on fares would yield a reduction, and the Regulator is unlikely to allow very rapid increases. Other parts of the industry have now been subject to careful profit maximisation in a highly competitive environment: marginal revenues are close to marginal costs and demand elasticities are high - so marginal revenues are close to fares. Bidding on fares will yield significant price reductions only if the bidders anticipate significant reductions in their marginal costs. This may be the case, but there do not seem to be large monopoly profits to be competed away. We would, however, concede that there is a middle ground, where services - for example, some InterCity services - are presently earning good profits which are used to cross-subsidise. Chadwick-Demsetz auctions could doubtless be made to work well in these cases.

In view of the complexities of rail privatisation and the political risks associated with things going wrong, it is necessary to have bidding arrangements which will be reliable. The Government's proposals probably meet this requirement. There is some reassurance in the considerable experience in a transport context of tendering for unremunerative bus services: bidding on minimum net cost with no fares control in some cases, and bidding on minimum gross cost (where fares revenues are irrelevant to the bidder) in other cases and in London. Hibbs notes that bus tendering is far from perfect,[1] but at least it demonstrates that a workable system is possible.

The Safety Factor

A worry is that the safety authorities may unexpectedly insist on some new feature that would increase the costs of operators or RailTrack. There might, for instance, be requirements to install automatic train protection, carry 'black boxes' or rebuild rolling stock to improve crash-worthiness. Such actions would risk voiding previously made contracts entered into in reasonable ignorance of the requirement. Compensation would be a way out, although the negotiation of the amount would be difficult and the Government would have to be persuaded to fund it.

Analysis of the economics of safety on the railways has not been particularly sophisticated. Privatisation presents an opportunity to rationalise some of the issues. The proposed system will throw into the open some costs of safety measures and make clear that they have to be paid for one way or another. There is an analogy with water, where the Director General of the Office of Water Services (OFWAT) is faced with financing the costs implied by the water quality standards imposed by outside bodies. He has opened a debate so that there is an opportunity to discuss whether the public is prepared to pay the cost of improved 'safety'.

7. London's Railways

LONDON IS VERY OFTEN given special treatment in new legislation because its size and administrative complexity make it genuinely different from elsewhere. Although London is not given special

---

[1] John Hibbs (1993), pp.62-65.

treatment in the rail privatisation Bill, it does raise particular issues.

The London area is the best place to start extensive franchising. In commenting on the nature of the various rail markets (page 18) we noted that the London area has, in many ways, the strongest markets. Passenger flows are dense, with less chance of long-term decline than elsewhere: rail is genuinely indispensable. Therefore, franchisees will have a clearer idea of their future revenues, especially if they can be given a firm commitment on the level of fares (which will certainly be regulated) in the future. Service patterns are complex and train paths are particularly interdependent, so that it is unrealistic to expect fundamental change in the short term. Little would therefore be lost if initial franchises confirmed current service patterns for a few years. There is relatively little complication due to the presence of freight services. Moreover, railway property is likely to be more valuable in the London area than elsewhere.

It is probably true, therefore, that complete privatisation of train operations and track ownership will be easier to achieve in the London area than elsewhere. This conflicts with the casual initial impression that the profitable InterCity business would be the easiest to privatise.

Privatisation in the London area will not, of course, be entirely straightforward. The Government has indicated that the Gatwick Express, currently operated by InterCity over Network SouthEast tracks, will be an early candidate for franchising. That will be an interesting test case because of the potential for strong competition for passengers between the several rail operators which will provide services in this corridor.

British Rail's present interests and responsibilities in the London area will be shared between a number of parties under the new proposals. Working agreements between London Transport (LT) and BR, two public bodies with similar duties and answerable to a single government department, may not be adequate in a more complex and commercial mixed régime. The separation of the Docklands Light Railway from London Regional Transport required agreements to be made in respect of Bank station at a cost of several hundred thousand pounds. There are six lines where one operator's services run over another's tracks. There are 16 stations which are jointly operated by

[51]

London Underground and British Rail, and 10 owned and operated by one operator but served by the other's services.

Genuine monopoly power is held by the railway in the London area. There is an explicit statement in the White Paper that the Government will wish to continue control of fares to stop them rising,[1] and will also wish to continue its attempt to enforce quantity and quality of service standards that are not necessarily what the commercial market would provide.

LT has an overall responsibility to co-ordinate with BR in providing public transport services for London. BR and LT have to consult on arrangements for fares and services within Greater London. The establishment of a franchising authority will have implications for LT's rôle since it will effectively set fares and service parameters for what is now Network SouthEast. It will be necessary as far as possible to make the Regulator's objectives and responsibilities consistent with those which presently govern London Transport. In particular, there could be real difficulties with London Transport's duty to co-ordinate public transport to meet London's needs: the more so if buses are deregulated. Revenue allocation between the London operators takes place now, but the principles involved might well have to be renegotiated if private sector operators and franchised services are included.

Joint London Transport and British Rail schemes such as CrossRail will create special problems. Some of them would have arisen sooner or later anyway under the present system because of divergent objectives and a need to share costs and revenues, some of which will, by design, have been diverted from other London Underground routes.

Some large rail investment schemes in the London area may pose other problems of co-ordination. To take an example, the Thameslink 2000 scheme shows a high estimated rate of economic return, because it provides faster access between the rail systems north and south of London and the employment generator in the centre. The economic benefits are generated by a holistic scheme which cuts across territories that will naturally form parts of quite separate rail franchises. If such a

[1] Cm.2012 (1992a), *op. cit.*, paras. 11 and 66.

scheme is to come to fruition, RailTrack will have to negotiate with the Franchising Director a long-term commitment to provide a stream of revenues against which the capital investment can be funded - perhaps with the help of a direct contribution from the Government. This will be considerably more difficult to arrange than in present circumstances in which many of the risks and issues like revenue abstraction are internalised by British Rail.

Ticketing Difficulties under Competition

Ticketing is a problem to be addressed throughout the country, but it is especially acute in the London area. Many problems of common or joint costs are repeated in the context of revenues. Attributable revenues may under- or over-exhaust total revenues. Existing revenue allocation mechanisms evade these problems by simply sharing the revenues in proportion to some such measure as passenger miles travelled on the respective systems.[1]

The White Paper mentions through- and joint-ticketing but says nothing about the mechanics of achieving it. It is, of course, a topic that consumed vast energies in the first 100 years of the railways' history. Systems of revenue clearing will have to be constructed and administered. The consultation document on franchising envisages that a 'Joint Industry Body will provide a forum for agreeing revenue apportionment and allocation mechanisms'. The body could become strife-torn and ineffective unless the Regulator imposes sensible principles for revenue sharing and has some means of enforcing the outcome on operators who can distort the process in their own interests - perhaps through the power to revoke licences.

The present British Rail models and systems of data collection for revenue allocation are imperfect. It may be that the electronic ticketing industry has become sufficiently mature to offer a better solution. Several operators, including London Buses and London Underground, are actively considering contactless, stored-value tickets. Just as London Transport insists that operators of their tendered bus routes must install electronic ticket-issuing equipment, so franchising may provide the ideal opportunity to overhaul ticketing systems. If the costs were

---

[1] The process is analogous to that of full-cost allocation.

justified, the information such systems would provide would be valuable for management, revenue sharing and regulatory purposes.

The Travelcard type of scheme, so popular with the public, can cause difficulties for competitive, commercial operations. To create sensible incentive systems, and to hold the interest of entrepreneurs, it will be necessary to resist the inevitable cries for ticketing systems that achieve vaguely defined benefits from 'integration' or 'co-ordination' at the price of removing a direct relationship between what the operator does and the cash he receives. Stored value, contactless ticketing may be a solution. Where revenue pools are established there will be problems similar to those which have arisen in the local bus industry of avoiding the creation of barriers to entry.

8. The New Proposals for the Railways: Political Issues

DEBATE ABOUT THE PRIVATISATION of the railways has been obscured by the exaggerated nature of opposing views. The Government has projected an attachment to an ideologically pure version of privatisation that probably exceeds its own hopes and expectations. Opponents of the policy have exaggerated the potential threats to the operation of an integrated railway. The functions of the several *dramatis personae* of the new railway world are crucial to the impact of privatisation.

The activities of regulators in other previously nationalised industries, such as gas, electricity and telecommunications, have generated immense public and political interest. Railways offer far greater scope for such interest. With other utility privatisations there was never a real chance that reform would lead to huge changes to the network of service provided or to the extent of provision on that network. Moreover, millions of ordinary citizens were offered a risk-free opportunity to make a small profit out of the process of selling the new shares. Because of changing supply conditions, the prices of gas and telecoms were able to fall significantly in real terms in the years after privatisation. Electricity charges to domestic users have not risen steeply, though water charges have risen to finance a huge (and much publicised) programme to catch up on investment, some of which has been attributable to outside requirements imposed by the EC.

Privatisations in some other industries, such as airports, steel, and Britoil, were different in that the industries were not providing monopoly (or virtual monopoly) services for the whole country. If privatisation had led to a large change in provision by these organisations, the overwhelming majority of the public would have remained unaware of the fact.

Economic Significance of Railway Services

But the railways do currently provide services in most of Britain. Most people use the network or feel that they may use it. Indeed, railways have a special significance (like motorways and international airports) because they are seen as an important feature in attracting investment to an area and sustaining accessibility to the nation as a whole. In the Canary Wharf case, for example, the developers quickly became aware that they would not be able to let their new office space unless a new railway linked it to central London. They would doubtless say that failure to provide the rail link in time caused the commercial failure of the project. Furthermore, people in Britain have an emotional attachment to railways that considerably exceeds their apparent willingness to pay for them. Thus, if privatisation were to result in any potential or actual reduction in the rail network or in levels of service, there would be a major political reaction. With electricity and water privatisation, security and quality of supply were taken for granted and controversies have concerned prices to the consumer. In railways price, quantity and quality of supply are all at issue.

The Regulator's and Franchising Director's duties imply relationships with the Government, with each other, with the owners and operators of the infrastructure, with owners and operators of trains, and with the public. In each relationship, there will be points that are politically contentious; badly-handled activities could threaten either the success of privatisation or the future of the railway system (or both).

The proper operation of a separate accounting system for identified train services will expose the cross-subsidies that currently exist within British Rail. For the first time, the public may be able to see which services make profits and which ones lose money (and how much). Inevitably, loss-making services will be seen as 'under threat'. Some services will, indeed, be seriously reconsidered when it is shown that each passenger carried receives a large subsidy.

To understand the full significance of this change it is necessary to

[55]

be aware of the way in which 'charging' has developed over the decades, into the 'prime user' system. In 1968 freight services were excused any infrastructure costs except where they were the only users of the infrastructure: that is, freight was only charged for infrastructure when it was the only and hence the prime user. Similarly, in the 1970s InterCity came only to bear infrastructure costs if it and freight alone used it. In cases where freight, InterCity and Provincial (now Regional) sectors shared infrastructure, the last was defined as the prime user and bore all the costs. The move to avoidable-cost-based charging (possibly with an additional margin depending upon what the markets will bear) will produce a radically different view of the relative economic performances of the sectors.

Establishing the Criteria for Subsidy

Closely related to the issue of profit- and loss-making services is the question of what criteria will be applied by the Franchising Director in deciding whether a particular service should receive subsidy. The Franchising Director will take responsibility for administering many hundreds of millions of pounds each year in subsidy to the railway. The principles for allocating the subsidy will have to be decided. Currently, the subsidy to British Rail lines is determined behind closed doors. Decisions reflect political criteria, of which one of the most important is negative - avoidance of closure. The Franchising Director will have to implement criteria for deciding which service gets what subsidy in accordance with instructions and guidance given by the Secretary of State. The Director will have to be prepared to explain publicly his reasons for not funding services when they have to be curtailed or withdrawn.

This procedure will mark a fundamental change in railway policy. Determination of such rules will be highly contentious. The cost-benefit techniques attempted under the 1968 Act were sound technically but failed to be implemented in practice. London Transport once developed 'passenger-miles per pound' criteria and Sir Peter Parker's proposal for the 'Social Fare' amounted to much the same thing.[1] Refinement is possible through systems of weights when

[1] P. Parker, *A Way to Run a Railway*, The Haldane Memorial Lecture, London: Birkbeck College, 1978.

giving credit for different types of travel to respond more flexibly to particular policy needs. The techniques are available but getting them agreed and making them operational will be a challenge.

The proposals for legislation will create new ways for the Government to extend political involvement into the proposed system in a way that allows for the political determination of the subsidy criteria. The Government might, for instance, attempt to influence RailTrack in the pricing of particular services to lower the cost of operating services on a line. Such action would amount to a hidden subsidy and would conflict with the criteria for subsidy used by the Franchising Director. It would also compromise the principle that RailTrack is to run a business without regard to non-commercial considerations which are to be dealt with by the Franchising Director.

Another political problem is that privatisation will lead to different charges being levied for the use of track in different parts of the country. Variations from one area to another will engender debates about 'fairness'. Unfortunately for politicians, many loss-making railway lines run through areas that are politically sensitive: either they contain marginal constituencies or safe ones (for the government of the day). The very process of identifying which lines make profits and which make losses, though laudable in terms of economic efficiency and open government, will create political pressures which may threaten privatisation.

Deciding the Total Subsidy

The total amount of subsidy is also a political issue. In the short term, there is no prospect of reducing subsidy because:

* productivity savings will take some time to come through;

* the backlog of investment must be caught up;

* future investment requirements must be financed; and

* reductions in profitability in some services because of regulation and, in the longer term, because of competition through open access, will imply replacement by direct subsidy.

If a Government chose, in the short term, to reduce subsidies in the new, 'marketised' system created by privatisation, the rail system

[57]

would have to contract. Lines would be closed and services would be cut back. 'Privatisation' would, wrongly, be blamed for such cuts.

Worse still, any need to pay for 'catching up' because of years of under-investment on the railways would be likely, if fed into the charges levied by RailTrack, to choke off potential interest in running services along lines that would, had the infrastructure been properly maintained, been attractive to new operators. The political problems here are intense: the 'market' solution after privatisation would be to raise subsidy via the Franchising Director to ensure that operators could profitably afford to pay for use of the infrastructure while paying sufficient to RailTrack to allow additional investment. Here again, the very openness caused by privatisation will generate new political pressures on the Government.

Privatisation will have several other politically important consequences. Once private companies provide some or all services there will inevitably be occasions when an operator goes bankrupt. In earlier privatisations of network services, such as gas and electricity, the financially buoyant and monopolistic nature of the enterprises meant that failure was unlikely. Even if a regional electricity company were to go bankrupt, new management could instantly step in to maintain supply. But with railways a company could go bankrupt (or cease trading for other reasons) in such a way that services ceased overnight, presenting a visible short-term threat to the integrated nature of the rail system and to the credibility of privatisation. The Railways Bill recognises this problem and makes provision for the appointment of temporary administration and for protection of the operating assets from creditors. The Franchising Director and the Regulator will have to decide what effort should be made to achieve 'security of supply' and at what cost, and the rôle for the skills and resources of a smaller (and shrinking) British Rail as a provider of last resort. They will, no doubt, recognise that strikes, technical failures and planned engineering works mean that security of supply is not absolute under the present system. This issue is important as the public may fear failure of supply, even if arrangements exist to avoid such an eventuality.

Similar potential problems arise because of the need to maintain through-ticketing facilities. In terms of public support or rejection, minor issues of this kind are likely to be most important. The Regulator will have to impose sensible principles for revenue sharing on the many operators providing train services (see above, page 53), and monitor the outcome to avoid cheating or distortions. The history of the Railway Clearing Houses provides an interesting pointer to the complex problems that may re-emerge.

9. Recommendations

Stimulating Change

AT SEVERAL POINTS we have questioned the degree to which the new proposals will actually allow change. The Government has retained several means of giving subsidies. With that possibility, there will inevitably be pressures to prevent change because there will be losers and the political or financial cost of placating them will be high. The Government has created a complex mechanism which may result in any one of a range of outcomes. At one extreme, there could be virtually no change from the present railway system and pattern of operation; at the other, Britain could end up with a wholly private-sector rail industry.

In the Government's view, RailTrack will become the leading institution in the industry. The corollary is that the industry's independence of government would be greatly helped by strengthening the independence of RailTrack. According to the Government, the intention is to privatise RailTrack, but not in the first instance. If RailTrack succeeds in meeting its proposed financial objectives, then it will be the most plausible candidate for privatisation on the established British model under the scrutiny of the Regulator. Essentially, RailTrack will be a large property company with a duty to use some of its property assets in a particular way. If it can break even, after earning a real rate of return on its railway investments, it will be possible to sell it at an early date because of the intrinsic value of the properties which can be exploited alongside or independently of the railway functions. Property has been an unattractive investment recently, but it will become much more appealing as the economy recovers - especially the kind of property, with good access to commercial centres, which will constitute the RailTrack portfolio.[1]

[1.] This proposition was advocated by Beesley and Littlechild (1983) in one of the earliest papers to discuss British Rail privatisation.

We have argued that it may be easier to achieve complete privatisation of the industry in the London area than elsewhere. Other methods of granting independence to RailTrack may be suggested, such as creating a Trust, as with the London Passenger Transport Board in 1933. It is for discussion as to whether such an alternative would be as effective as private ownership.

The Franchising Director, choosing which services to support at one remove from the final passenger, and RailTrack making maintenance and investment decisions at two removes, risk blunting the impact of any market-driven pressure for change. Interestingly, Sweden, which has also separated track from train operations, has opted for an approach in which operators themselves ask for track access to provide for services which *they* define.[1] Under the British proposal, it is possible to define and let franchise contracts in a spirit which either denies all opportunities to the bidding operators to suggest 'non-compliant' innovations or which rewards them for doing so. Bureaucratic barriers to the market can be lessened by the latter approach.

One of our concerns is the potential for political interference in the move to a more market-driven railway. Doubtless the Government currently intends to maintain a hands-off approach. But there is a lack of popular understanding of what is proposed within rail 'privatisation'. The public is woefully ill-informed about the issues involved. Ignorance will breed political problems as the new arrangements start to operate. Only then will the Government feel pressured to use the many levers and pulleys available to it. There have been several examples in recent years (notably the poll tax) of policies which failed partly because government did not consider the political implications. Ministers must heed the warnings of such earlier failures.

The Creation of Two Agencies

Some commentators have questioned the decision to create two separate agencies, the Regulator and the Franchising Director. There seem to be enough separate tasks to keep both busy. There will be danger in having the two agencies only if there are unnecessary conflicts created by differing objectives or functions.

[1] We are grateful to J.-E. Nilsson for this observation.

Certainly, there are areas where duplication of effort could usefully be avoided. In particular, both agencies will need access to the management information and the models which will allow them to estimate avoidable costs, revenues and profits. There are very few analysts already familiar with these matters; it will be difficult and expensive for others to acquire a working knowledge of them. Thus, it may well be sensible to set up a common pool of expertise. Similar comments may apply to legal and other professional skills. For instance, the Regulator has to approve the outline form of the contracts to be made between the Franchising Director and the operators. Is it necessary for each agent to have his own independent advice?

But these arguments are secondary. In our view, only the Regulator stands a real chance of establishing and preserving independence from government from the very beginning, simply because he will not be directly responsible for the spending of public money. Such grounds alone are sufficient to justify the establishment of a regulatory office, distinct from the Franchising Director. However, we have also stressed the immensely complex nature of the world in which the Regulator and the Franchising Director will be operating. Politics will encourage the blunting of accountability as to who is responsible for what. It is our view that independence for the Regulator and for the Franchising Director (of both the Government and other interests) is crucial to making rail privatisation work.

The Need to Make Funding Credible

It is clear to everyone, including the Government, that rail privatisation proposals will be accepted only if MPs and the electorate are convinced that the level of state financial support (and thus services) will be maintained, at the very least until revenues increase or cost efficiencies are achieved. The Government has stated this to be its intention. However, in the current public expenditure climate there is a problem of credibility. As Figure 1 (above, page 16) shows, the November 1992 Statement has the External Financing Limit for British Rail falling from £2,000 million in 1992-93 to £1,432 million, £1,000 million and £853 million in the following three years (at constant 1992 prices, assuming 4 per cent inflation). London Transport has suffered a similar cut in funding.[1] No doubt there are explanations for the fall in the planned future EFL - for example, completion of Channel Tunnel-related investment, an expectation of economic recovery leading to a recovery in revenues and property sales, and so on - but these explanations ought to be made in the context of the rail privatisation proposals.

The Government is currently showing itself to be shy of committing itself to full funding of public transport investment schemes, such as the Channel Tunnel Rail Link, CrossRail, refurbishment of the Northern Line and Thameslink 2000. Some way must be found for the Government (and specifically, the Treasury) to give a credible promise that privatisation will not be used as an opportunity to cut rail funding in the short term. Moreover, the public will wish to see estimates of the size of the individual budgets allocated to the several types of subsidy payments which we have identified. Similarly, it would be helpful to publish rough estimates of the magnitude of the efficiency gains and cost savings which are expected. Without them no individual or organisation will have a means of assessing how he or she will be affected.

The future funding of rail, particularly state subsidy, is currently an area of almost total obscurity. Lack of clarity means that opponents of rail privatisation proposals will, entirely reasonably, be able to encourage public concern about the system in general and, more importantly, about particular lines and services. A secure commitment to funding levels for the existing railway, coupled with estimates of efficiency gains and cost savings, is vital both to public acceptance and to generating private interest in running services.

10. Conclusions

Rail privatisation was never going to be easy. There is a vast difference between what the Government is currently attempting to do to the railways and the privatisation of, say, water or electricity. With most recent state sell-offs, buyers were queuing up and there was no likelihood that, because of privatisation, service would cease to be provided. Railways have few certain private providers, while

[1] See Glaister and Travers (1993), for more detail.

[62]

there is a clear risk that the openness of the franchising process will generate economic pressures to close lines or reduce services.

In the same way that Ministers tend to exaggerate the degree of change and the possible benefits of change, opponents of rail privatisation have overplayed many potential difficulties of reforming the railways. Indeed, the opposition to rail privatisation has attacked the policy on several grounds which boil down to a single problem: a changing political environment. The process of publishing the costs of operating particular services, private operator comment about the dire state of the infrastructure, surpluses and deficits on particular services, and several other results of 'privatisation' will indeed lead to new pressures on the railway. Most of these pressures will come because of increased openness about the condition, costs and benefits of the railways which may, in turn, lead to a debate about whether less (or more) should be spent on Britain's railway system. Privatisation or franchising of the railways could produce benefits in terms of improved productivity, better management and lower costs. These benefits could mean either lower subsidy or higher service standards or both.

The political nature of the privatisation process is hard to exaggerate. This paper has sought to point out some key areas where the Government may have underestimated the political consequences of its proposals, or where it is most unlikely that politicians will refrain from intervening in ways which undermine the effective operation of the proposed new system. The Regulator, RailTrack and the Director of Franchising will each operate in a highly public and a highly political environment where decisions could lead to difficulties for the Government. 'Privatisation' will be blamed by opponents for every minor failure of the system. As a result, Ministers will seek to intervene to protect themselves.

Such Ministerial intervention could seriously damage the benefits accruing from the new organisation of the railways. It will pay the Government to explain clearly the likely consequences of its policies. That is, the exposure of the subsidies necessary to keep operating particular services; the possibility that ticketing arrangements could be radically altered; and new arrangements for ensuring continuity should all be laid out as potential consequences of the reform. The benefits anticipated in terms of better services and lower subsidies could then be weighed against the perceived costs.

[63]

An informed and open discussion should take place before the start of the creation of the new market for railways. If it does not, the Government risks losing the debate without it ever having taken place.

References

Beesley, M.E. and S.C. Littlechild (1983): 'Privatisation: principles, problems and priorities', *Lloyds Bank Review*, No.149.

Beesley, M.E. and P.B. Kettle (1985): *Improving Railway Financial Performance*, Aldershot: Gower.

Bös, D. (1993): 'Privatisation in Europe: a Comparison of Approaches', *Oxford Review of Economic Policy*.

Department of Transport (1992a): White Paper, *New Opportunities for the Railways*, Cm.2012, London: HMSO, July.

Department of Transport (1992b): *The Franchising of Passenger Rail Services*, DoT Consultation Document, October.

Department of Transport (1993): *Gaining Access to the Railway Network*, DoT Consultation Document, February.

Dodgson, J. (1993?): 'Railway Privatisation', in M. Bishop, J.A. Kay, and C.P. Mayer (eds.), *Privatisation*, Oxford: Oxford University Press (forthcoming).

Foster, C.D. (1992): *Privatization, public ownership and the regulation of natural monopoly*, Oxford: Blackwell.

Friedlaender, A.F., *et al.* (1993): 'Rail costs and Capital adjustments in a quasi-regulated Environment', *Journal of Transport Economics and Policy*, May.

Glaister, S. (ed.) (1987): *Transport Subsidy*, Newbury, Berks.: Policy Journals.

Glaister, S. and T. Travers (1993): *Meeting the Transport Needs of the City*, City Research Project, Corporation of London, March.

Hibbs, J. (1993): *On the Move...: a Market for Mobility on the Roads*, Hobart Paper No.121, London: Institute of Economic Affairs.

Jones, I., P. Marks, and C. Willis (1993): *Franchising Passenger Railway Services*, London: NERA.

Joy, S. (1973): *The Train That Ran Away! A Business History of British Railways 1948-1968*, London: Ian Allan.

Nash, C. and J. Preston (1992): *Barriers to Entry in the Railway Industry*, Institute for Transport Studies, Leeds University.

On the Move...
A Market for Mobility on the Roads
JOHN HIBBS

This *Hobart Paper* addresses one of the great economic and social problems of our time: the suboptimal allocation of resources that has arisen from incompatible financial, fiscal and regularity régimes for the various modes of inland transport. In order to simplify the argument, it concentrates on the movement of people, whose demand for access to satisfactions gives rise to the derived demand for mobility with which the paper is concerned. The argument rests on the assumption that such satisfactions can only be assessed subjectively and that there is no planning technique which will ensure the provision of the required mobility at a quality and price which will clear the market.

Despite the emotional and atavistic interest in railed transport which confuses transport policy debate, the paper centres on the use of roads for travel, regarding the private car in this context as 'just another form of transport'. Failure to recognise this by the public transport industry is due mainly to protectionist regulation of the bus and coach industry from 1930 to 1985. A pivotal issue, however, is the irrationality of the investment and fiscal régimes for roads. The paper stresses the advantages to be gained from electronic road-use pricing, which would enable the bus to become, as it should be, a complementary mode to the private car.

Having reviewed the various 'means to mobility', the paper concludes that measures to harmonise their investment, taxation and regulatory régimes so as to create an integrated market form the basis for the only 'national transport policy' that can have either meaning or success.

ISBN 0-255 36319-2   Hobart Paper 121

 The Institute of Economic Affairs
2 Lord North Street, Westminster
London SW1P 3LB
£8.95   Telephone: 071-799 3745

Federalism and Free Trade

JEAN-LUC MIGUÉ

Protectionism has become less and less of a viable instrument of intervention by national governments, particulary for member-states of common markets. This *Hobart Paper* provides a formal framework for analysing the effect on domestic policy choices of constraining the power of national governments to maintain trade barriers, as experienced in GATT-type arrangements, in common-market treaties, and in other freer-trade agreements within blocs of trading partners. The author, Professor Jean-Luc Migue of the University of Quebec, argues that the government of a national economy with free inward and outward movement of factors and goods, has little or no power to engage in purely redistributive policies. The member governments of a common market are in a position approximating that of the government of a small economy, free of trade barriers. Federalism and free trade go hand in hand inasmuch as they both strenghten governments' power to do good, while restricting their power to abuse citizens.

The paper attempts to show that the opening of national frontiers to freer movement of goods, services, capital, and people will result in less use of other instruments of intervention in domestic affairs. Less reliance on protectionism by national governments will have an impact similar to reinforcing devolution of power within federal states. Imposing heavier taxes and restrictive regulations on national resources in conditions of free trade leads first to more rapid and more pronounced substitution of foreign for local production. It also causes capital to move out of higher-cost economies. Finally, victims of government abuse may 'vote with their feet' and leave the territory. Freer trade is a first step and a sufficient condition towards the federalisation of the world.

However, this competitive federalist model only works if national and local decisions are not superseded by vast central powers covering the same fields within trade blocs or at the supra-national level. As a tool for cartelising national and regional governments, centralisation weakens the ability of citizens to escape unpopular measures by moving their goods or their production factors to more favourable locations and uses.

ISBN 0-255 36320-6

Hobart Paper 122

The Institute of Economic Affairs
2 Lord North Street
London   SW1P 3LB
Telephone: 071-799 3745

£7.95